# A-MAZE-ing
## Western National Parks & Monuments

Rising Moon

# Hang On!

These Mount Rushmore inspectors are all tangled up!
Follow their ropes and help them find out which president they will be inspecting.

# Right on Time!

It's a gusher! Can you find your way out of the boiling water erupting from Old Faithful Geyser?

# Climb Through Time

Jeff wants to study millions of years
of geologic history in Grand Canyon National Park.
Help him climb down through the layers all the way
to the mighty Colorado River.

START

Kaibab Limestone

Toroweap Formation

Coconino Sandstone

Hermit Shale

Supai Group

Redwall Limestone

Muav Limestone

Bright Angel Shale

Tapeats Sandstone

Vishnu Schist

FINISH

# Gotta Go!

It's an emergency! Emily needs to weave her way through this campsite at Yosemite National Park to the restrooms at the other end. Can you help her? Hurry!

# Moose Madness

These moose are in a mess!
Find a path through their antlers from the start to the finish.

# Get Along Lil' Doggie

Help! This poor prairie dog must find which tunnel leads to his cozy den below before the hungry hawk snatches him up.

JONES

# Where the Buffalo Roam

Mama! Somehow in Yellowstone Park, Baby Buffalo got separated from his mom.
Lead him through the herd to the top of the hill so she won't have to worry much longer.

START

# Leave it to Beaver

Help this hungry beaver make it up Archangel Cascade
to the tasty looking tree at the top.

# Little Lost Lamb

Baa Baa! Guide this little lost lamb down Canyon de Chelly
to his wooly buddies sipping water below.

# Saddle Up Partner

Find the correct path that leads to Phantom Ranch.
Watch out for scorpions and dead-end trails.

# Step on a Crack...

Watch your back! These happy-go-lucky ants may not be so lucky
if the greedy lizard can get to them without stepping on a mud crack.

# Old Faithful Won't Wait!

Walk along the boardwalks to meet your friends at Old Faithful. Watch out for animals, tourists, or repairs blocking the way.

START

# Checkmate!

Guide this bighorn sheep down
Checkerboard Mesa without stepping
on a line. Be careful. It's steep.

Start

Finish

# Home Sweet Hole in the Tree

This nutty resident of Yosemite has collected enough food
to last through the winter. Can you help him squirrel his stash away
in his nest hidden in the trees?

# Hoodoo?

Can you? Help the mule deer wind her way from top
to bottom through the tall spires of Bryce Canyon.

FINISH

# Giddy-Up!

This lonely horse needs a guide to lead him from
Spider Rock to the rain cloud looming above.
Can you help him?

# Stranded!

It's so hot you can fry an egg on a rock! Help these stranded tourists make it back to Scotty's Castle, a cool oasis in the middle of the desert.

DEATH VALLEY DUNES

BADLANDS

FINISH

RACETRACK PLAYA

SCOTTY'S CASTLE

START

# Something's Fishy!

It's a feisty one! Follow each fisherman's line to his catch.
Who caught the prize Snake River Cutthroat?

Rainbow Trout          Brook Trout          Snake River Cutthroat          Brown Trout

# King of the Castle

Guide this little rabbit through the maze of corn to the cool,
refreshing creek below Montezuma Castle.

# Take a Hike!

Put on your hiking boots and start climbing! Can you make it from the bottom of Sentinel Rock all the way to the top?

# River Runners

Whoa! Splash! Ride these raging
Colorado River rapids without running into a logjam or
tipping over on a rock.

**FINISH**

# Happy Trails

Ready. Set. Go! Hike your way from the North Rim to the South Rim and rest in the Grand Canyon Village.

# Close Encounters

Far Out! Soar through this mess of UFOs to the bottom
of the tower, safe and sound back on earth.

# Peek-A-Boo!

Hidden inside a giant saguaro is this tiny elf owl's nest.
Can you help him find his way back home?

# It's a "Snow-Down!"

On the count of three start skiing! Which one of these cross-country skiers will make it back to Jackson Hole?

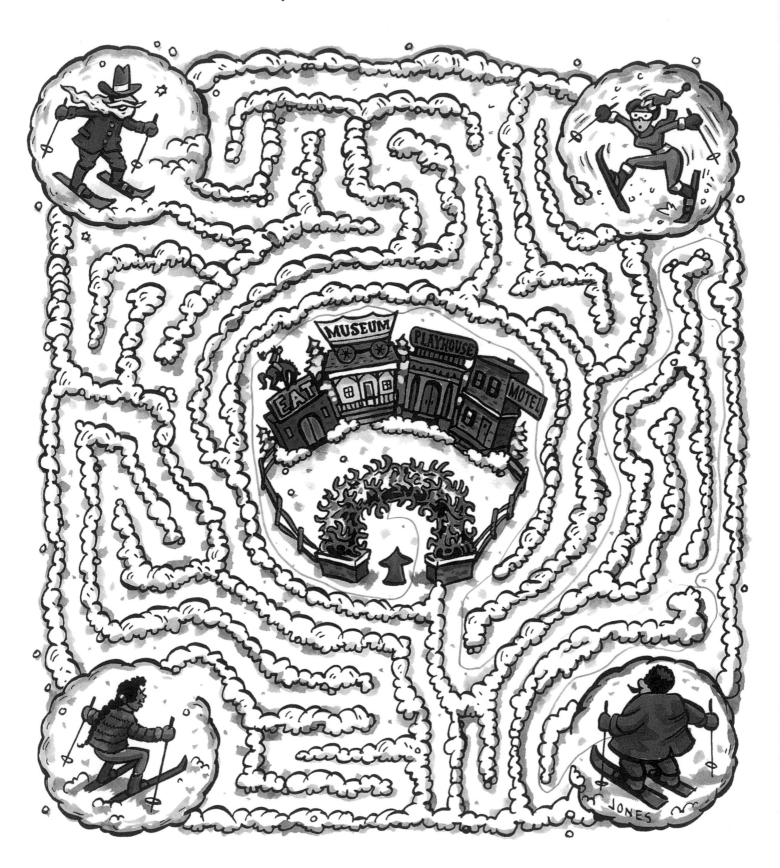

# Coyote Blues

Ow Oww Owww! Help these howling coyotes sing a duet together under the light of the moon on top of Blue Mesa.

# Blinded by the White

Can you help this white mouse find a path through
the sand dunes of White Sands National Monument?
There might be some shade under those yuccas.

FINISH

# Under and Over

Can you make it under three of these sandstone arches
and over the famous Delicate Arch?

*Clue: Go under one of the arches twice, and avoid any poisonous creatures along the way.*

# How Far to El Tovar?

After a long day of hiking in the Grand Canyon, you want to know one thing: which one of these trails leads to the El Tovar Hotel?

# Animal Tracks

These animals have left their tracks behind.
Match the bison, the coyote, the elk, and the bear with the correct set of tracks.

# That's Nutty!

Sandy the Squirrel knew her nuts would be safe in the Petrified Forest,
but now she can't find them! Can you help her?

# Don't Get Stuck!

Lead these hikers through Saguaro National Park to the setting sun.
Bonus: Can you find the deer, coyote, javelina, and mountain
lion hidden in the park?

START

FINISH

# Bear Trouble

Don't feed the bears in Yellowstone Park!
Can you make it all the way back to your tent
without disturbing a single bear?

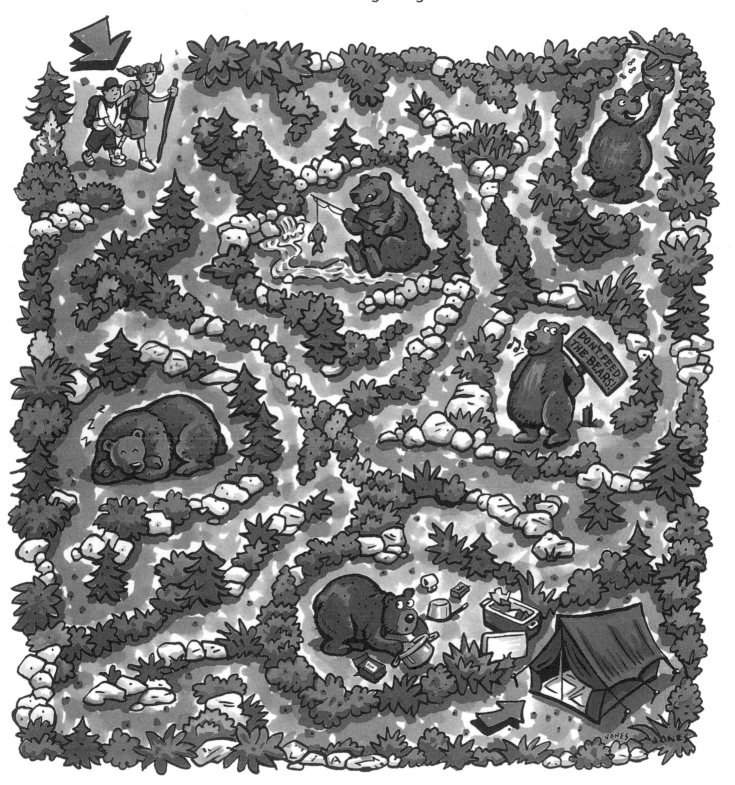

# Dino Dig!

Don't step on any dinosaur bones as you wind through
this paleontological site to reach your tent.

# Photo Safari

Smile pretty for the camera. Find a path that leads to each of these animals found in the Grand Tetons without retracing your steps.

# Batty!

Lead this bat through the windy tunnels
and nooks of Carlsbad Caverns to the open evening air,
where bugs and other delectables are aplenty.

# Step Right Up!

Climb the ladders and scale the walls as you venture
into the ruins of Mesa Verde from one end to the next.
Don't pick up any ancient artifacts along the way!

# The View from the Top

Help this lizard reach his friend at the top of the tower.
The view from up there is sensational!

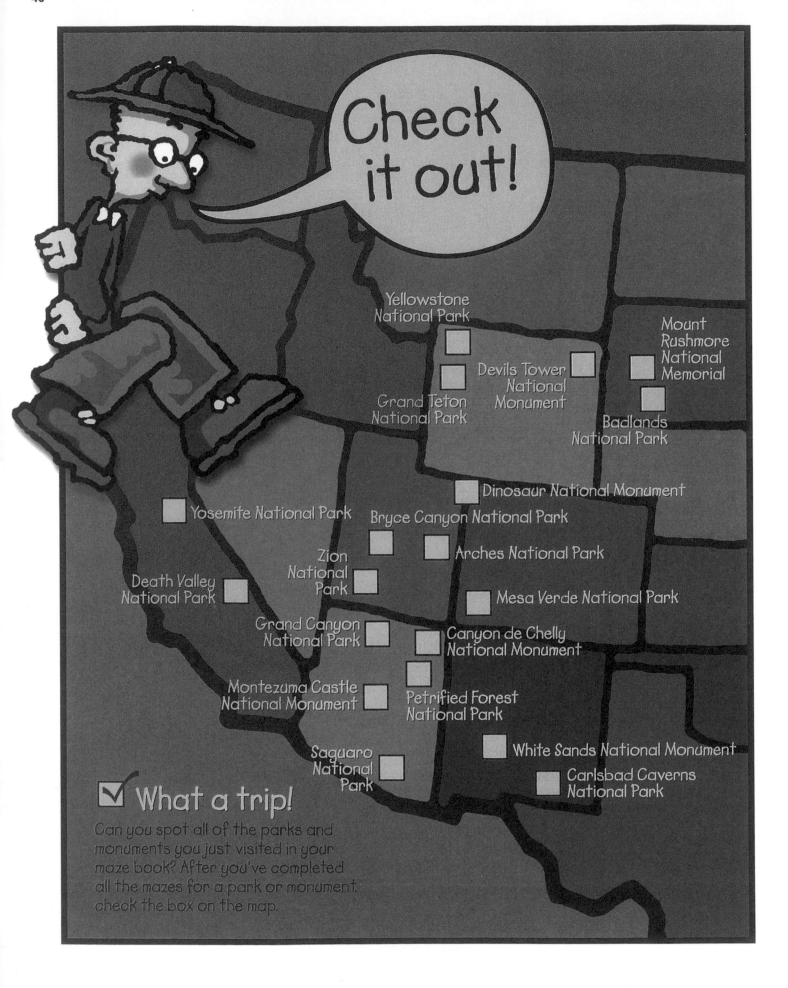

# Fun Facts

**Yosemite National Park,** California—
*established October 1, 1890*
Yosemite National Park has the
most granite domes in the
world, including the world's
largest granite monolith,
El Capitan. The park also contains
Yosemite Falls, the world's fifth
highest waterfall, and forests of giant
sequoias, the world's largest living things.

**Mount Rushmore National Memorial,**
South Dakota—*established March 3, 1925*
Washington's, Jefferson's, Roosevelt's, and
Lincoln's heads are each 60 feet tall,
about the same size as a ponderosa pine
tree. Theodore Roosevelt's mustache is
20 feet across, about the length of
two cars bumper to bumper.

**Yellowstone National Park,** Wyoming—
*established March 1, 1872*
Yellowstone National Park is the first and oldest
national park in the world. The park contains the
famous Old Faithful Geyser. Approximately every 76
minutes, the geyser erupts, expelling gallons and
gallons of boiling water into the air. The park also
contains some 10,000 hot springs and geysers, the
majority of the planet's total.

**Devils Tower National Monument,** Wyoming—
*established September 24, 1906*
Devils Tower is known as Bears Lodge to several
northern plains tribes. According to legend, seven
little girls climbed up on a rock to get away from
a bear. The rock then rose to the sky and the
girls turned into stars. The bear tried to climb
up the huge rock, but slid, leaving his claw
marks down the whole tower, making Devils
Tower the way we know it today.

**Death Valley National Park,** California—
*established October 31, 1994*
Summer temperatures in Death Valley average
115 degrees. One of the highest recorded temperatures in the United States was recorded in
Death Valley—134 degrees on July 10, 1913.

**Petrified Forest National Park,** Arizona—
*established December 9, 1962*
The fossilized trees found in the Petrified
Forest were once live trees that were
buried after they died. Sediments,
minerals, and ash began to replace
the cells of the tree, turning the trees
into brightly colored stone.

**Bryce Canyon National Park,** Utah—
*established September 15, 1928*
Water, ice, and wind are the forces that shape the
colorful and unusual spires at Bryce Canyon into
what are called *hoodoos.*

**Zion National Park,** Utah—
*established November 19, 1919*
Zion is a Hebrew word that means a place of safety
or refuge. Mormon pioneers gave the canyon this
name in the 1860s.

**Grand Canyon National Park,** Arizona—
*established February 26, 1919*
The Grand Canyon used to be called Bucareli Pass.
Later, the name was changed to Big Canyon, until
eventually the official name
became what we are now
familiar with, Grand Canyon.
Today, people from all over
the world come to gaze
into the canyon, which in
some parts is over one mile
deep. All that work was
created by the Colorado
River, slowly cutting its way
along the bottom.

**Grand Teton National Park,** Wyoming—
*established February 26, 1929*
The Grand Teton towers more than a mile above the valley of Jackson Hole. Twelve of the Teton peaks are over 12,000 feet tall (that's like 8 Empire State Buildings stacked one on top of the other). Plus, the peaks support a dozen mountain glaciers.

**Saguaro National Park,** Arizona—
*established October 14, 1994*
A saguaro cactus can live to be 150 years old. A mature saguaro can grow to a height of 50 feet and weigh over 10 tons (that's more than what two adult elephants weigh together).

**Badlands National Park,** South Dakota—
*established November 10, 1978*
The Lakota called the Badlands "mako sica." Early French animal trappers knew the area as "les mauvaises terres a traverser." Both mean "bad lands," which eventually became the official name of this dry, rugged area in South Dakota.

**Arches National Park,** Utah—
*established November 12, 1971*
There are over *two thousand* arches in Arches National Park, including the world famous Delicate Arch.

**Mesa Verde National Park,** Colorado—
*established June 29, 1906*
For hundreds of years people lived in communities in and around Mesa Verde, which means "green table" in Spanish. They lived in stone villages in the sheltered alcoves of the canyon walls. Although there have been many theories as to why the people who built the beautiful structures at Mesa Verde left their homes, their disappearance still remains a mystery.

**Montezuma Castle National Monument,** Arizona—*established December 8, 1906*
Montezuma Castle is not a castle and Montezuma, an Aztec emperor in Mexico, was never there! Early settlers thought the five-story, 20-room cliff dwelling must have been made by a king. Because of this, they misnamed it Montezuma Castle, even though it was abandoned almost 100 years before the Mexican emperor was ever born.

**Canyon de Chelly (Shay),** Arizona—
*established April 1, 1931*
People have been living in Canyon de Chelly with its red cliffs, petroglyphs and cliff dwellings for more than 1,500 years. Spider Rock stands tall at the bottom of the canyon. In Navajo belief, Spider Woman, who taught humans the art of weaving, lives among the rocks.

**Carlsbad Caverns National Park,** New Mexico—
*established May 14, 1930*
Carlsbad Caverns National Park contains 100 known caves, including the nation's deepest and third longest limestone cave. Around one hundred years ago, explorers used to lower themselves into the caverns in huge buckets to collect bat droppings to use for fertilizer.

**Dinosaur National Monument,** Colorado—
*established October 4, 1915*
The Quarry Area of Dinosaur National Monument contains some 1,600 exposed bones from eleven different dinosaur species, such as Stegasaurus, a gigantic creature with the brain the size of a walnut.

**White Sands National Monument,** New Mexico—
*established January 18, 1933*
Many of the animals that reside in White Sands National Monument have evolved to be white, which allows them to blend in with the white gypsum sand.

# Answers

## Page 2—Hang On!

## Page 3—Right on Time!

## Page 4—Climb Through Time

## Page 5—Gotta Go!

## Page 6—Moose Madness

## Page 7—Get Along Lil' Doggie

50

Pages 8 & 9—Where the Buffalo Roam

Page 10—Leave it to Beaver

Page 11—Little Lost Lamb

Page 12—Saddle Up Partner

Page 13—Step on a Crack...

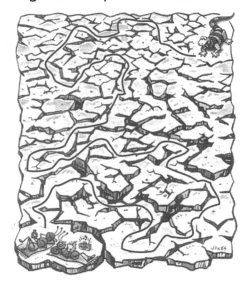

51

Pages 14 & 15—Old Faithful Won't Wait!

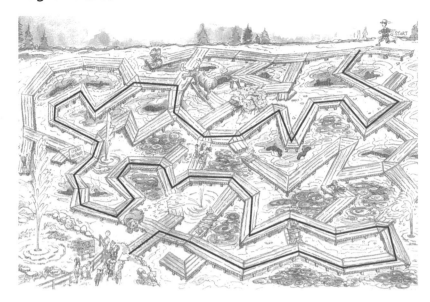

Page 16—Checkmate!

Page 17—Home Sweet Hole in the Tree

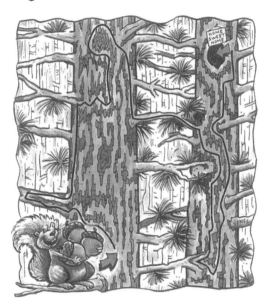

Page 18—Hoodoo?

Page 19—Giddy-Up!

52

Pages 20 & 21—Stranded!

Page 22—Something's Fishy!

Page 23—King of the Castle

Page 24—Take a Hike!

Page 25—River Runners

Pages 26 & 27—Happy Trails

Page 28—Close Encounters

Page 29—Peek-a-Boo!

Page 30—It's a "Snow Down!"

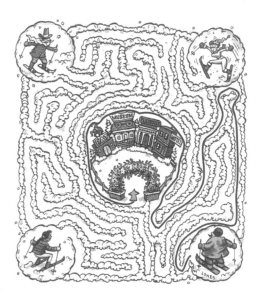

Page 31—Coyote Blues

Page 32—Blinded by the White

Page 33—Under and Over

Pages 34 & 35—How Far to El Tovar?

Page 36—Animal Tracks

Page 37—That's Nutty!

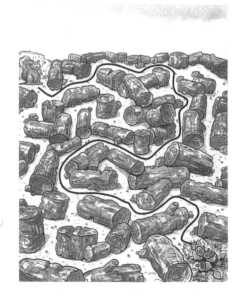

## Page 38—Don't Get Stuck!

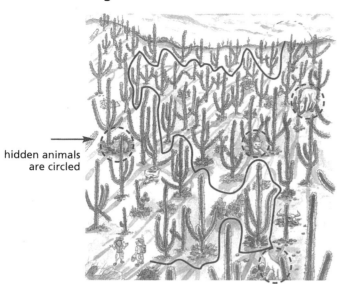

hidden animals
are circled

## Page 39—Bear Trouble

## Pages 40 & 41—Dino Dig!

## Page 42—Photo Safari

## Page 43—Batty!

## Page 44—Step Right Up!

## Page 45—The View from the Top

Text © 2002 by Rising Moon
Illustrations © 2002 by:
    Larry Jones, pp. 2, 7, 13, 17, 22, 25, 30, 32, 37, 39, 42, 45
    Joe Marciniak, pp. 5, 12, 14-15, 20-21, 28, 34-35, 38
    David Brooks, Cover art, pp. 3, 4, 10, 19, 24, 29, 31
    Peter Grosshauser, pp. 6, 11, 18, 23, 33, 36, 43
    Bill Perry, pp. 8-9, 16
    Joe Boddy, pp. 26-27, 40-41
    Beth Neely & Don Rantz, pg. 44

www.risingmoonbooks.com

Composed in the United States of America
Printed in Johor Bahru, Malaysia   June 2015

Edited by Theresa Howell
Production by Chantelle Call
Production supervised by Donna Boyd
For more fun facts go to www.nps.gov

FIRST IMPRESSION 2002